November 2009

THE TRAINER STANDARDS POCKETBOOK

By John Townsend

Drawings by Phil Hailstone

"At last a practical, portable book for everyday use by busy trainers and for all those managers who provide occasional training and presentations."
Peter Gallwey, Consultant, GM Development SARL.

"John Townsend has done it again! I doubt whether you'll ever find so much on all aspects of training for trainers, in such a concise and easily understandable format."
Steve Pallay, Recruitment, Training and Career Development Manager, Caterpillar Overseas S.A.

CONTENTS

HOW TO USE THE STANDARDS

This pocketbook has been built from the trainer performance standards of Team Training International. These standards were developed by **John Townsend** and **Maurice Lewis** in an attempt to provide an international, free-thinking group of trainers with challenging but easy-to-use measures of professionalism (see also the 'Acknowledgement' on page 93).

HOW TO USE THE STANDARDS

MISSION

Training is a noble and rewarding profession because it is dedicated to helping people grow.

By developing people's skills, increasing their knowledge or positively influencing their attitudes, trainers contribute daily to individual self-esteem and collective effectiveness.

In order to maintain the integrity of their profession, trainers need high standards of ethics and conduct.

These standards have been developed as an easy-to-use checklist to measure this professionalism. They can be used as a:

- **Performance appraisal aid**
- **Self-evaluation tool**
- **Checklist for each training programme**

HOW TO USE THE STANDARDS

SCOPE

Bodies and groups, boards and committees have produced excellent phone-book-thick 'bibles' of standards and other guidelines for the training function.

This is a pocketbook for daily use by trainers and their bosses.

It is to be carried around and consulted by people whose principal task is to TEACH training programmes. For this reason, the standards have been divided into three sections and cover only the basic, generic part of the trainer's job:

1 **Creating/adapting** training programmes
2 **Preparing** for training programmes
3 **Animating** (giving life to/delivering) programmes

Definitions: A **Programme** is broken down into **Modules** (autonomous learning topics) and **Sessions** (periods between breaks).

HOW TO USE THE STANDARDS

PERFORMANCE APPRAISAL

To use these standards as a performance appraisal aid, trainers and their boss should:

- Firstly, agree on which of the standards apply to the job; in some cases they may disagree with a standard or find it too high or too low

- Then they should agree to delete, lower or raise it - or find another one; these standards cover most aspects of an 'on-line' trainer's job (not that of a training manager, course developer or training administrator) but every job is different

- Next, the trainers should agree to have their boss or a third party observe their performance and evaluate it against these standards

- Lastly, the trainers and their boss should discuss how well the standards have been met and agree on an action plan to bring up to standard any inadequate performance

SELF-EVALUATION

Even if your job as a trainer covers more than just creating/adapting and delivering training programmes, you will find here some pretty challenging yardsticks with which to measure your performance in these areas.

Every 3-6 months, glance through this pocketbook and ask yourself: 'Am I honestly meeting these (or other self-imposed) standards when I design and/or deliver a programme?'.

If not, why not? After examining your various excuses, set objectives for bringing your performance up to standard. Where applicable, action ideas are included with the standard.

THE STANDARDS

These standards were developed as a tool to help a group of international trainers agree on '**What does a professional trainer do?**'.

Most trainers do not have the time to read - or even the spare energy to carry around - the currently available tomes on trainer standards.

These standards are challenging, precise, observable, measurable. As such, they are wide open to disagreement. **Please disagree - but provide an alternative which is just as precise, observable and measurable!**

Each page of each of the three sections contains a standard for one element of trainer performance. Sometimes this standard is broken down into components. Wherever possible simple action ideas on how to meet the standard are included on the page, next to the [ACTION] logo. See the 'self-study suggestions' section for full references to any books and tapes listed.

HOW TO USE THE STANDARDS

TRAINER QUALIFICATIONS

In order to meet the professional standards of performance outlined in this pocketbook, trainers will, of course, have mastered the subject matter of the programme they are teaching. In addition, they will have acquired, through study, training or experience, a testable, working knowledge of up-to-date concepts for the following areas:

- Training Needs Analysis
- Training Programme Objective-setting
- Training Programme Evaluation
- Presentation Techniques
- Psychology of Influence and Persuasion
- Principles of Creative Problem-solving

- Group Facilitation
- Principles of Communication
- Time Management
- Learning Theory/Practice
- Training Hardware and Technology

See page 90 for 'self-study suggestions'

NOTES

8

CREATING/ADAPTING TRAINING PROGRAMMES

CREATING/ADAPTING TRAINING PROGRAMMES

CRITERIA

Whether professional trainers are responsible for creating and animating new programmes or for animating existing programmes, they must at least be aware that a good training programme meets the criteria below.

A professionally designed programme takes into consideration **5 phases**:

1   Assessing the need for training
2   Designing the framework of the programme
3   Developing the content of the programme
4   Animating the programme (bringing to life and delivering it)*
5   Evaluating the results of the programme

* See chapter 4 (page 57) on standards for animation

NEEDS ASSESSMENT

WHY?

Before developing and/or animating a programme, professional trainers know why it is needed. They can answer the question: 'What, specifically, is happening/has happened to justify running a programme?'.

- Read 'How to Measure Training Effectiveness'

- Consult with senior management as to discrepancies between plans and results

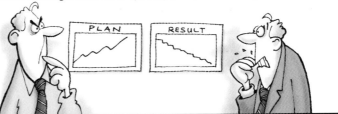

CREATING/ADAPTING TRAINING PROGRAMMES

NEEDS ASSESSMENT

WHAT?

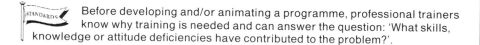

Before developing and/or animating a programme, professional trainers know why training is needed and can answer the question: 'What skills, knowledge or attitude deficiencies have contributed to the problem?'.

- Read 'How to Measure Training Effectiveness'

- Participate in/lead a competency-based training needs analysis

CREATING/ADAPTING TRAINING PROGRAMMES

NEEDS ASSESSMENT

WHO?

Before developing and/or animating a programme, professional trainers know who has been selected to attend. They can answer the questions: 'How were they selected? What are their backgrounds? What are their individual needs? What range of needs exist in the group?'.

- Read 'How to Measure Training Effectiveness'

- Participate in/lead a competency-based training needs analysis

- Ask for (and record on flip chart) participants' needs as an icebreaker at the beginning of each course

PROGRAMME DESIGN

OBJECTIVES

Before developing and/or animating a programme, professional trainers can specify what specific skills, knowledge or attitude changes will have taken place by the end of the programme and how those changes will be measured.

- Read 'Preparing Instructional Objectives'

- Practise using the future perfect tense for objectives (ie: 'At the end of this course, participants will have ....') and asking, 'What will I accept as evidence that they have ....?'

CREATING/ADAPTING TRAINING PROGRAMMES

PROGRAMME DESIGN

OUTLINE

 Before developing and/or animating a programme, professional trainers can produce a 1-2 page outline that specifies:

- Programme objectives (see previous page)
- Programme modules (autonomous learning topics)
- The breakdown of modules into sessions (periods between breaks)
- What kind of exercises will be used to allow participants to practise their newly acquired skills, knowledge or attitudes
- When and where the programme should be conducted

CREATING/ADAPTING TRAINING PROGRAMMES

PROGRAMME DESIGN
CHECKLIST/BUDGET

Before developing and/or animating a programme, professional trainers can produce an overall checklist for everything that will be required to run the programme. This should include:

- People needed/involved
- Training materials and equipment
- Training room requirements

If practicable, an estimated cost figure can be given for these requirements.

CREATING/ADAPTING TRAINING PROGRAMMES

PROGRAMME DEVELOPMENT
INTRODUCTION

Before animating a programme, professional trainers make sure that it contains an introductory module covering at least the following:

- The programme rationale (Why? What? Who?)
- The programme objectives (specific changes expected)
- The programme outline and schedule
- Expected roles/behaviours of participants and trainer

CREATING/ADAPTING TRAINING PROGRAMMES

PROGRAMME DEVELOPMENT

INCLUSION ACTIVITIES

Before animating a programme, professional trainers make sure that it contains an inclusion activity (icebreaker) at the beginning of each day.

- Consult one of the many published collections of icebreakers for new ideas

- Develop own ideas for icebreakers and test them with a control group of colleagues first

CREATING/ADAPTING TRAINING PROGRAMMES

PROGRAMME DEVELOPMENT
LEARNING POINTS

 Before animating a programme, professional trainers make sure that no module contains more than **5** learning points without a linking memory device of some kind (donkey-bridge).

- Watch 'Memories are Made of this' (video tape)

- Practise creating memory devices for complex learning points (acronyms, slogans, rhymes, logos, etc)

PROGRAMME DEVELOPMENT

MEDIA/METHODS

STANDARDS — Before animating a programme, professional trainers make sure that there is a change of medium or teaching method at least every 10 minutes (ie: that training sessions call for the successive use of different visual aids, varied types of practical exercises, etc).

ACTION

- Read 'The Trainer's Pocketbook'

- Watch 'Ten Training Tips' (video tape)

PROGRAMME DEVELOPMENT

LEARNING STRUCTURE

Before animating a programme, professional trainers make sure that, for each learning point, there is:

- An explanation/discussion
- A demonstration (example, analogy, demo)
- An exercise for participants to practise the new learning
- A guidance/correction activity

(21)

CREATING/ADAPTING TRAINING PROGRAMMES

PROGRAMME DEVELOPMENT
LEARNING REINFORCEMENT

STANDARDS Before animating a programme, professional trainers make sure that it is structured in such a way that key learning points are repeated and used as a basis for the next step of the teaching.

(This 'linking of learning' provides the reinforcement necessary to changes in behaviour, knowledge and attitude.)

PROGRAMME DEVELOPMENT

TRAINING MATERIALS

Before animating a programme, professional trainers ensure that all training materials (visual aids, handouts, etc) meet the 'Preparation of Support Devices' standards on pages 45-54.

ACTION

- Read 'The Trainer's Pocketbook'

- Practise! Get to the training room 90 minutes early and use a checklist

PROGRAMME DEVELOPMENT
BREAKS

Before animating a training programme, professional trainers check that there are breaks planned at least every 90 minutes.

● Break! No excuses

CREATING/ADAPTING TRAINING PROGRAMMES

PROGRAMME DEVELOPMENT

RECAPS

 Before animating a programme, professional trainers ensure that there is a recap or review of learning planned for each **module** (autonomous learning topic).

- Work on inventing creative recap devices such as quizzes, tests, group competitions, etc

- See the Pocketfiles of ready-to-use-exercises in the Management Pocketbooks Series

PROGRAMME DEVELOPMENT
SLOW/RELUCTANT LEARNERS

Before animating a programme, professional trainers make sure that they have a contingency plan for slow or reluctant learners.

● Read 'The Challengers Pocketbook'

● Raise the question with your boss or the participants' department head and plan what to do in the event of such problems

PROGRAMME EVALUATION
REACTION LEVEL 1

Prior to animating a programme, professional trainers make sure that some device exists for obtaining on-going feedback from participants **during** the programme (to allow them to modify or adjust, in the case of misdirection of any kind).

- Use 'spot checks' (see 'The Trainer's Blue Pocketfile of ready-to-use exercises')

- Conclude each day with a round-table feedback session

CREATING/ADAPTING TRAINING PROGRAMMES

PROGRAMME EVALUATION
REACTION LEVEL 2

STANDARDS Prior to animating a programme, professional trainers check that there is an evaluation cycle planned which includes a device to measure participants' reactions **at the end** of the programme.

ACTION
- Read 'Evaluating Training Programs at 4 levels'

- Read 'Training Needs Analysis and Evaluation'

CREATING/ADAPTING TRAINING PROGRAMMES

PROGRAMME EVALUATION
LEARNING LEVEL (PRE/POST TEST)

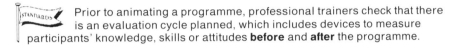 Prior to animating a programme, professional trainers check that there is an evaluation cycle planned, which includes devices to measure participants' knowledge, skills or attitudes **before** and **after** the programme.

● Read 'Evaluating Training Programs at 4 levels'

● Read 'Training Needs Analysis and Evaluation'

PROGRAMME EVALUATION
BEHAVIOURAL LEVEL (TRANSFER)

Before animating a programme, professional trainers make sure that there is an evaluation cycle planned, which includes devices to measure how well participants have applied the new skills, knowledge or attitudes as a result of the programme.

- Use at least 2 of the following devices:

  - 360° questionnaires (participants, peers, boss, subordinates)
  - review of action plans created during training
  - 360° interviews (participants, peers, boss, subordinates)
  - observation of participants' use of learning

- Read 'Evaluating Training Programs at 4 levels' and/or 'Training Needs Analysis and Evaluation'

CREATING/ADAPTING TRAINING PROGRAMMES

PROGRAMME EVALUATION
RESULTS LEVEL

 Before animating a programme, professional trainers make sure that (if applicable) there is an evaluation cycle planned which at least **attempts** to measure changes in organisational results following the programme.

- Read 'Evaluating Training Programs at 4 levels'

- Read 'Training Needs Analysis and Evaluation'

NOTES

PREPARING FOR TRAINING PROGRAMMES

PREPARING FOR TRAINING PROGRAMMES

THE STAGES

Professional trainers should be responsible for the preparation of every programme - **however many times they have run it before**. Preparing to run a programme concerns not only the training 'environment' but also the mental and physical preparation of the trainer.

This responsibility for preparation has been divided into 3 sections:

● Trainer preparation

● Preparation of training environment

● Preparation of programme materials, equipment and support devices

TRAINER
ARRIVAL TIME

Professional trainers arrive at the training site at least one hour before the start of the programme.

TRAINER

PHYSICAL AND MENTAL PREPARATION

Professional trainers take at least 15 minutes before the arrival of the first participant to prepare themselves **physically and mentally** for the programme.

- **Physical preparation**
  Centre energy; prepare grooming, posture and breathing; relax

- **Mental preparation**
  Visualise the participant group; try to imagine how they are feeling; ask yourself: 'How can I best help these people to change and grow, given the programme objectives and the organisational culture?'

PREPARING FOR TRAINING PROGRAMMES

TRAINER
CHECKLIST

Professional trainers always have a checklist itemising all the materials, equipment, etc, needed for the programme and which they personally carry to the training site.

TRAINER
PERSONAL ENERGY

 Professional trainers consciously manage their personal energy level by avoiding temptations to over-eat, over-drink and under-sleep, both before and during the programme!

TRAINER

FITNESS

 Professional trainers keep physically fit with at least one type of exercise per week.

ENVIRONMENT

 Professional trainers decide on or influence the choice of the venue and/or training room, using the following criteria:

- 5 square metres approx. per participant

- Controllable heating and ventilation

- Minimum 500 lux lighting

- Enough sockets or extension leads for electrical equipment

- Adequate catering arrangements

ENVIRONMENT
MAIN ROOM

Professional trainers take personal responsibility for the set-up of the main training room and its subsequent impact on learning.

- Arrange desks/tables and chairs to fit programme style (see 'The Trainer's Pocketbook')

- Check availability and suitability of wall space for display purposes

- Check access to fire exits

PREPARING FOR TRAINING PROGRAMMES

ENVIRONMENT
GROUP ROOMS

 Professional trainers take personal responsibility for the location and set-up of group/syndicate rooms and their subsequent impact on learning.

- Negotiate and secure availability of **nearest possible** group rooms at **earliest possible** date before programme is to be run

- Check equipment and material in each room at least one hour before programme starts

ENVIRONMENT

CATERING

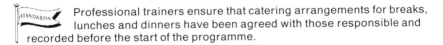

Professional trainers ensure that catering arrangements for breaks, lunches and dinners have been agreed with those responsible and recorded before the start of the programme.

- Insist on coffee/tea being available slightly **before** scheduled breaks!

- Wherever possible insist on 'buffet' style, self-service meals to save time and allow choice on quantity

- Wherever possible avoid alcohol being served at lunch

PREPARING FOR TRAINING PROGRAMMES

ENVIRONMENT
RELATIONS WITH STAFF

 Professional trainers **visibly** and **audibly** demonstrate respect for all support staff.

PREPARING FOR TRAINING PROGRAMMES

SUPPORT DEVICES
OVERHEAD PROJECTOR

 When an overhead projector is to be used, professional trainers:

- Position projectors and screen to maximise visibility for all participants

- Check focus and size of image on screen

- Check projector for spare lamp

- Tape projector mains lead to floor or provide other protection against tripping

SUPPORT DEVICES

TRANSPARENCIES

Professional trainers prepare transparencies which meet the **FLICK** standards:

- Each has a standard *horizontal* **F**rame

- Each has large **L**ettering (titles: 1-2 cm high; text: 0.5-1 cm high)

- Each has at least one **I**mage, Icon or Illustration

- Each uses at least one **C**olour more than black

- Each has been **K**ISSed! (key words only - 1 topic only - six lines maximum - six words per line maximum)

- Watch 'Ten Training Tips' (video tape)

PREPARING FOR TRAINING PROGRAMMES

SUPPORT DEVICES
FLIP CHART

 When a flip chart is to be used during the programme, professional trainers:

- Ensure there are enough flip chart stands in main and group rooms

- Prepare enough paper for whole programme

- Check all markers and change dry ones

- Prepare in advance all necessary sheets (see also page 84 for standards on flip chart use)

(47)

SUPPORT DEVICES
35MM SLIDE PROJECTOR

When a 35mm slide projector is to be used during the programme, professional trainers:

- Practise dimming room lights

- Test visibility of images at various levels of lighting and select the best conditions

- Check and test **all** slides for correct alignment in the carousel

- Insert 'black' slides at appropriate points

SUPPORT DEVICES
WHITEBOARD

When a whiteboard is to be used during the programme, professional trainers:

- Clean off any previous and/or irrelevant material from board

- Check all markers for whiteboard suitability and 'hide' wrong ones

SUPPORT DEVICES
PINBOARD

When a pinboard (talking wall) is to be used during the programme, professional trainers:

- Ensure that there are enough backing sheets for the whole programme

- Check that there is an ample supply of pins, spray glue or post-its

- Check that there are enough cards, dots and markers for all exercises

SUPPORT DEVICES
CASSETTE/CD PLAYER

 If background music or sound effects are to be used, professional trainers:

- Check batteries/mains lead and test volume

- Check all cassettes/discs and cue effects so that they are ready for 'immediate' play

- Tape any leads to the floor or provide other protection against tripping

PREPARING FOR TRAINING PROGRAMMES

SUPPORT DEVICES
VIDEO PLAYER AND MONITOR

If video tapes are to be shown during the programme, professional trainers:

- Check all tapes for correct functioning

- Ensure video monitor is switched to correct channel and cue all tapes to start immediately on 'play'

- Ensure that leads are taped to the floor or otherwise protected against tripping, etc

PREPARING FOR TRAINING PROGRAMMES

SUPPORT DEVICES

VIDEO CAMERA

If a video camera is to be used during the programme, professional trainers:

- Test camera for proper functioning and play a test tape back through the monitor

- Check microphone for proper functioning; if external, check battery

- Ensure that there are enough blank tapes for all exercises and participants

- Always carry a spare microphone battery

PREPARING FOR TRAINING PROGRAMMES

SUPPORT DEVICES
HANDOUTS

When handouts are to be distributed during the programme, professional trainers:

- Ensure that the text has been typed in an easy-to-read type face (eg: Times, Helvetica, Courier, Palatino, Bookman, Garamond and New Century)

- Ensure that text, layout and graphics follow professional principles

- Ensure that the level of reading complexity fits the participant group

- Prepare the material chronologically and stack for ease of use

PREPARING FOR TRAINING PROGRAMMES

WELCOME

 Before participants arrive in the training room, professional trainers:

- Distribute prepared participant name cards to fit programme objectives

- Place relevant handouts and other material on each participant's table

- Display a 'Welcome to .....' visual aid (flip chart, transparency, etc)

NOTES

ANIMATING TRAINING PROGRAMMES

ANIMATING TRAINING PROGRAMMES

FIVE KEY AREAS

Training programmes must be brought to life - animated - not just delivered!
Animation is the primary responsibility of professional trainers and covers:

- Ethics and Attitude
- Use of Support Devices

- Presentation Skills
- Timing

- Facilitation Skills

- For several standards in this section it is suggested that feedback be
  provided by a co-trainer as well as by participants

ANIMATING TRAINING PROGRAMMES

ETHICS AND ATTITUDE
MISSION

Professional trainers have committed themselves verbally or in writing to the **Mission** (or an equivalent one) on page 2.

ETHICS AND ATTITUDE

 Professional trainers handle their own and participants' opinions and beliefs with tact and discretion. They are aware that every individual has a different notion of truth and reality. If asked, no participant will be able to cite a hurtful example of disrespect on the part of the trainer.

ACTION
- Ask for co-trainer feedback

- Ask for participant feedback

- Video tape yourself

ANIMATING TRAINING PROGRAMMES

ETHICS AND ATTITUDE
EXERCISES

 Professional trainers organise and manage exercises to encourage participant success and use any apparent failure as feedback for participant development. There is, therefore, no evidence during a programme that participants feel they have been tricked, embarrassed or humiliated.

- Ask for co-trainer feedback

- Ask for participant feedback

- Video tape exercises for later assessment

ETHICS AND ATTITUDE

HELPING PHILOSOPHY

Professional trainers truly believe that their role is to help and facilitate rather than control and dominate. They will, therefore, have communicated their philosophy **overtly** to the participant group at least once during the programme.

● Ask for participant feedback

ETHICS AND ATTITUDE

PERSONAL OPINIONS

 Professional trainers **never** use a training programme as a platform for giving personal views or opinions that are unrelated to the programme objectives. No participant, therefore, will make any critical remark to this effect, either to the trainer or to a third party.

- Ask for co-trainer feedback

- Ask for participant feedback

- Video tape yourself

ANIMATING TRAINING PROGRAMMES

PRESENTATION SKILLS
EYE CONTACT

 Professional trainers establish sensitive 'lighthouse' contact with each participant - moving round the room but not staring at anyone for longer than **2 seconds** unless in dialogue.

- Ask for participant feedback

- Ask for co-trainer feedback

- Video tape yourself

ANIMATING TRAINING PROGRAMMES

PRESENTATION SKILLS
VOICE

 Professional trainers:

- Project their voice so all can hear

- Articulate words and pauses between words

- Avoid repetitive verbal 'tics'

- Modulate their voice for interesting 'light and shade' and make use of pauses

- Vary the speed of their delivery

- Ask for co-trainer feedback

- Audio or video tape all or parts of your presentation; set yourself specific 'voice' objectives

ANIMATING TRAINING PROGRAMMES

PRESENTATION SKILLS

BODY

 Professional trainers:

- Take note of feedback to ensure that their body language is congruent with their messages

- Use open gestures and avoid 'closed' body positions at all times

- Avoid distracting mannerisms such as: jangling change/keys in pockets; playing with markers/notes; 'swaying'; perching dangerously on furniture; etc

 • Ask for co-trainer feedback

- Video tape yourself   • Set objectives

PRESENTATION SKILLS

HUMOUR

 Professional trainers:

- Encourage participants to laugh, ensuring that there is at least one outburst of laughter per session

- React with humour to their own mistakes

- Record (audio or video tape) a session

- Ask for co-trainer feedback as to how funny you really are!

(67)

ANIMATING TRAINING PROGRAMMES

FACILITATION SKILLS
CREATING AN OPEN ATMOSPHERE

Professional trainers create an open atmosphere during a training programme by ensuring that each participant has expressed at least one opinion by the end of the first half day.

- Use an interactive icebreaker

- Arrange for an early discussion/case study exercise

- Organise a round table 'Why I am here' presentation

ANIMATING TRAINING PROGRAMMES

FACILITATION SKILLS
POSITIVE REINFORCEMENT

Professional trainers use positive reinforcement when responding to 4 out of 5 participant interventions.

- Get into the habit of giving a verbal 'receipt' for all contributions

- Don't be obsequious, but thank all contributors - even the seemingly aggressive ones; use your own style

- Read 'The Challengers Pocketbook'

ANIMATING TRAINING PROGRAMMES

FACILITATION SKILLS
HANDLING OBJECTIONS

 Professional trainers reflect **all** objections back to the speaker to check understanding before answering. In 3 out of 5 cases, they deflect the answer to the group or to an individual participant for handling.

- Start reflections with 'In other words, you're saying ...' or 'Let me see if I've understood ...'

- Read 'The Challengers Pocketbook'

ANIMATING TRAINING PROGRAMMES

FACILITATION SKILLS
NON-VERBAL MESSAGES

Professional trainers take account of specific non-verbal messages from participants and are seen to react immediately to at least 2 such messages per session.

- Read 'Bodily Communication'

- Practise observing and interpreting body language in trains, buses, airports, etc

ANIMATING TRAINING PROGRAMMES

FACILITATION SKILLS
ANECDOTES, METAPHORS, PARABLES

Professional trainers illustrate **each** of their training messages with at least one anecdote, metaphor or parable.

- Watch 'Memories are Made of this'

ANIMATING TRAINING PROGRAMMES

FACILITATION SKILLS
CHECKING LEARNING

 Professional trainers test/check participants' learning (at least once per module) with regular closed questioning sessions, tests or quizzes.

 • Create a number of varied recap devices for each of your courses (for helpful ideas see also the Pocketfiles of ready-to-use exercises in the Management Pocketbooks Series)

ANIMATING TRAINING PROGRAMMES

FACILITATION SKILLS
BRAINSTORMING

 When leading brainstorming sessions, professional trainers:

- Record **all** ideas without evaluation

- Encourage 'crazy' ideas which may trigger others

- Help the group to select the best idea

- Use the 5-point voting method to select best ideas: each participant has 5 points to allocate in **any way** they wish without voting for any of their own ideas!

NB The brainstorming method should only be used when the trainer has no preference/teaching bias for any solution.

ANIMATING TRAINING PROGRAMMES

FACILITATION SKILLS
DISCUSSION LEADING

When leading 'learning discussions', professional trainers use the
Socratic method. This means sharing and channelling participants'
ideas/answers into a suitable learning format (handout, checklist, mnemonic,
flip chart display, etc) - without being accused of manipulation!

- Prepare teaching points

- Ask **open** questions, such as 'Now what do you all think about ...?'

- Paraphrase and re-formulate answers to fit in with your teaching points

- Add your own points when necessary

- Summarise the process on a flip chart/pinboard

ANIMATING TRAINING PROGRAMMES

FACILITATION SKILLS
OPEN QUESTIONS

When leading 'learning discussions', professional trainers ask **open** questions as opposed to closed ones.

Closed questions have only one answer; open questions have many:

- 'What do you think about ...?'
- 'How could we ...?'
- 'Why ...?'
- 'What would you do if ...?'

FACILITATION SKILLS
PROCESS/PROGRAMME CHANGES

Professional trainers communicate each process or programme change by using a support device (see pages 82-88).

NB This is to avoid unnecessary confusion and wasted time/energy caused by misunderstood instructions or arrangements.

FACILITATION SKILLS
SKILLS EXERCISES: 1

 Professional trainers organise 'skills-practising' exercises by designating at least one **observer** for each 'round' of practice.

(The only exception to this standard applies to two-person exercises where the subject is confidential. For example: listening, coaching, counselling exercises.)

ANIMATING TRAINING PROGRAMMES

FACILITATION SKILLS
SKILLS EXERCISES: 2

Professional trainers organise 'skills-practising' exercises in such a way that no participant complains of him/herself or others:

- being confused
- being humiliated
- not understanding what was expected
- being unfairly overstretched
- being manipulated
- being victimised

ANIMATING TRAINING PROGRAMMES

FACILITATION SKILLS
SKILLS EXERCISES: 3

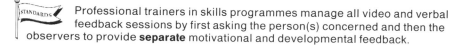

Professional trainers in skills programmes manage all video and verbal feedback sessions by first asking the person(s) concerned and then the observers to provide **separate** motivational and developmental feedback.

Suggested feedback model:

● Ask person(s) practising new skills for their own evaluation

● Watch video or recap on exercise

● Give feedback:
  Motivational - What, specifically, was good and why?
  Developmental - What, specifically, could be improved, why and how?

FACILITATION SKILLS
GROUP EXERCISES (GENERAL)

Professional trainers manage group exercises by leaving groups to work alone while monitoring attention to task.

81

ANIMATING TRAINING PROGRAMMES

USE OF SUPPORT DEVICES

 The professional trainer will use at least 3 support devices per session.

USE OF SUPPORT DEVICES
OVERHEAD PROJECTOR

 When using an overhead projector, professional trainers:

- Use pre-prepared and sorted transparencies in sleeves

- Place transparencies and align them before switching on

- Position themselves so as not to block anyone's view

- Use a paper 'mask' where applicable to reveal lists one point at a time (but show whole message first)

- Build complex messages by overlaying non-framed foils onto the original transparency

- Use a non-rolling pointer to highlight items

- Switch off projector between transparencies

(83)

ANIMATING TRAINING PROGRAMMES

USE OF SUPPORT DEVICES
FLIP CHART

 When using a flip chart, professional trainers:

- Maximise visibility for **all** participants
- Give each sheet a title
- Write for a max of 10 seconds before turning back to group
- Use at least **2 dark** colours
- Ensure messages are legible from 10 metres
- Avoid sentences
- Flip over (or 'tear and display') when learning point is finished

- Read 'Graphics for Presenters'
- Watch 'Ten Training Tips'

ANIMATING TRAINING PROGRAMMES

USE OF SUPPORT DEVICES
WHITEBOARD

 When using a whiteboard, professional trainers:

- Test all markers for whiteboard suitability before writing

- Erase data when it is no longer relevant

- Adhere to all applicable flip chart standards (page 84)

ANIMATING TRAINING PROGRAMMES

USE OF SUPPORT DEVICES
CASSETTE/CD PLAYER

When using music or sound effects, professional trainers:

- Prepare and cue each consecutive CD/tape track before hitting 'play'

- Keep player volume at a non-irritating level (no complaints!)

ANIMATING TRAINING PROGRAMMES

USE OF SUPPORT DEVICES
35MM SLIDE PROJECTOR

 When using a 35mm slide projector, professional trainers:

- Darken the room to a pre-prepared level **before** showing first slide

- Keep an ambient light on for notes, and so that they can be seen by participants

- Wherever possible avoid showing slides during the 1½ hours following lunch

ANIMATING TRAINING PROGRAMMES

USE OF SUPPORT DEVICES
VIDEO TAPES

 When using video tapes to support their messages, professional trainers:

- Introduce the tape by explaining where it fits into the learning structure of the programme

- Lead a discussion immediately following the showing in order to 'fix' learning

- Avoid showing video tapes during the 1½ hours following lunch

TIMING

Professional trainers keep their time promises (including time for questions and discussions).

• Always start on time after breaks, even if some participants are absent; this shows respect for the good timekeepers and encourages late comers to be on time next time

89

SELF-STUDY SUGGESTIONS

BOOKS

- Management Pocketbooks
  (Several titles in this series, including 'The Challengers Pocketbook', will
  provide useful additional reading)
- 'The Learning Company'
  Pedlar, Burgoyne and Boydell, McGraw Hill, 1991
- 'Improving Trainers' Effectiveness'
  Edited by Dr. Roger Bennett, Gower, 1988
- 'How to Measure Training Effectiveness'
  Leslie Rae, Gower, 1991
- 'Preparing Instructional Objectives'
  Robert Mager, Kogan Page, 1990
- 'The Adult Learner - a neglected species'
  Malcolm Knowles, Gulf Publishing, 1990
- 'Evaluating Training Programs at 4 levels'
  Donald Kirkpatrick, ASTD Books, 1995
- 'Training Needs Analysis and Evaluation'
  Frances and Roland Bea, IPM Books, 1994

BOOKS (continued)

- 'Journal of the Institute of Personnel Development'
- 'Influencing with Integrity'
  Genie Laborde, Syntony Publications, 1987
- 'Use Your Head'
  Tony Buzan, BBC Publications, 1976
- 'Accelerated Learning'
  Roger G Swartz, EMIS, P.O. Box 1607, Durant, OK 74702, USA
- 'The Dinosaur Strain'
  Mark Brown, Element Books, 1989
- 'The Psychology of Interpersonal Behaviour'
  Michael Argyle, Pelican, 1981
- 'Group Power'
  William Daniels, University Associates, 1990
- 'Graphics for Presenters'
  Lynn Kearney, 5379 Broadway, Oakland, CA 94618, USA
- 'Bodily Communication'
  Michael Argyle, Methuen, 1988

SELF-STUDY SUGGESTIONS

AUDIO AND VIDEO TAPES

Audio

- 'Tips for Trainers'
  John Townsend, Management Pocketbooks, 1991
- 'Creative Training Techniques'
  Bob Pike, Resources for Organisations, 1994
- 'Supercreativity'
  Tony Buzan, Audio Renaissance, 1988

Video

- 'Ten Training Tips'
  John Townsend, Melrose Film Productions, 1994
- 'Memories are Made of this'
  John Townsend, Melrose Film Productions, 1994
- 'Ideas into Action'
  Mark Brown, Melrose Film Productions, 1993

About the Author

John Townsend, BA, MA, MIPD

John is Managing Director of the Master Trainer Institute. He founded the Institute after 30 years of experience in international consulting and human resource management positions in the UK, France, the United States and Switzerland.

From 1978-1984 he was European Director of Executive Development with GTE in Geneva with training responsibility for over 800 managers in some 15 countries. Mr Townsend has published a number of management and professional guides and regularly contributes articles to leading management and training journals.

In addition to training trainers, he is also a regular speaker at conferences and leadership seminars throughout Europe.

Contact:

John Townsend can be contacted at:
The Master Trainer Institute, L'Avant Centre,
13 chemin du Levant, Ferney-Voltaire, France
Tel: (33) 450 42 84 16   Fax: (33) 450 40 57 37
E-mail: john.townsend@wanadoo.fr

First published in 1995 by Management
Pocketbooks. Reprinted 1998, 2000
All rights reserved. © John Townsend

Printed in England   ISBN 1 870471 27 X

Acknowledgement:

Many thanks to Bill Daniels, Hubert König and Finn Gomnaes of Team Training International for their invaluable help in developing the original standards.

Team Training International - with offices in Austria, Benelux, Czech Republic, Denmark, France, Germany, Hungary, Norway, Russia, Slovakia, Slovenia, Sweden, Switzerland, Ukraine, UK and USA - can be reached at: Isbarygasse, 12, A-1140 Vienna.
Tel: (43) 1 94 05 110   Fax: (43) 1 94 05 1111

ORDER FORM

Your details

Name _____

Position _____

Company _____

Address _____

_____

_____

Telephone _____

Facsimile _____

E-mail _____

VAT No. (EC companies) _____

Your Order Ref _____

Please send me:

No. copies

The ___Trainer Standards___ Pocketbook ☐

The _____ Pocketbook ☐

The _____ Pocketbook ☐

The _____ Pocketbook ☐

The _____ Pocketbook ☐

Order by Post

MANAGEMENT POCKETBOOKS LTD
14 EAST STREET ALRESFORD HAMPSHIRE SO24 9EE UK

Order by Phone, Fax or Internet
Telephone: +44 (0)1962 735573
Facsimile: +44 (0)1962 733637
E-mail: pocketbks@aol.com
Web: www.pocketbook.co.uk

Customers in USA should contact:
Stylus Publishing, LLC, 22883 Quicksilver Drive,
Sterling, VA 20166-2012
Telephone: 703 661 1581 or 800 232 0223
Facsimile: 703 661 1501 E-mail: styluspub@aol.com